Original title:
Under the Roof of Dreams

Copyright © 2025 Creative Arts Management OÜ
All rights reserved.

Author: Julian Prescott
ISBN HARDBACK: 978-1-80587-160-6
ISBN PAPERBACK: 978-1-80587-630-4

Reveries Between the Beams

The cat thinks he's a king, and struts,
On the rafters high, no room for doubts.
A mouse plays tag with a bit of string,
While I'm just here trying not to sprout.

In the Atrium of Possibility

An old shoe shines like a treasure chest,
With secrets whispered from days of rest.
I call it art, my masterpiece,
Though it smells like something I can't digest.

Where Dreams Find Their Wings

My dreams take flight on a paper crane,
But they forgot to pack the good champagne.
They loop and dive with little grace,
While I just sit here, grinning insane.

Mosaic of Midnight Whispers

The clock ticks loudly, a mocking tune,
While I'm lost in thoughts of a dancing raccoon.
Stars giggle softly at my silly plight,
As I chase shadows that vanish too soon.

The Sanctuary of Hidden Thoughts

In a nook where giggles grow,
A whisper tickles, don't you know?
Pillow forts and secret schemes,
Each hidden thought dances in dreams.

Chasing shadows, laughter loud,
Forming plans beneath a shroud.
With socks as swords and hats for crowns,
We ride the waves of make-believe towns.

The Quilt of What Could Be

Stitched together with bright red threads,
Imaginary tales in our heads.
Patchwork patches of joy and spree,
Cuddle up, it's wild as can be.

Under stars of our design,
Count the sheep, sip on sweet brine.
Make a catapult from a shoe,
Launch dreams far, just me and you.

The Labyrinth of Idea and Fantasy

Wandering paths of candy cane,
Here a dragon, there a train.
Ideas sprout like daisies wild,
Each corner hides a dreaming child.

Oh look! A talking toaster sings,
Dancing jellybeans on bright springs.
What's that? A pizza speaks in rhymes,
Welcome to our world of funny times.

Voices Behind Closed Windows

Shh, can you hear the giggles there?
Voices floating on the air.
Tickling tales that bend and twist,
Witty words we can't resist.

Open a curtain, peer inside,
Where logic bends and dreams abide.
Through those panes, a circus roams,
Making every room feel like a home.

When Wishes Take Flight

A chicken dreams of flying high,
She tries to leap, but just a sigh.
Her friends all cluck and cheer her on,
While pigs roll laughing 'til the dawn.

A cat claims he's a mighty knight,
With paper hat, he's quite the sight.
He fancies mice within his quest,
But they just want to take a rest.

The Haven of Slumbering Thoughts

In the land where pillows dance at night,
Dreams wear pajamas, oh what a sight!
The teddy bears argue about their roles,
While nightlights giggle, spinning in shoals.

A sock thief lurks in the moon's bright beams,
His heist of footwear creates silly dreams.
When one pair's missing, chaos unfolds,
As slippers plot coups, oh, the joy it holds!

A Dome of Enchanted Visions

A frog in a crown gives orders grand,
He rules the pond, it's quite the land.
His subjects croak in synchronized glee,
While fireflies dance like they're on TV.

The shadows waltz beneath the night,
As stars play hopscotch, what a delight!
The sky's a stage, and dreams take turns,
As laughter warms like a thousand suns.

Ciphers of the Moonlit Haunt

A ghost named Fred can't find his way,
He trips on sheets, what a display!
With all his moans, he spooks a few,
But ends up laughing, who knew, who knew?

In shadows lurk bizarre creatures' dreams,
With twisty tails and laugh-out-loud schemes.
They mingle and giggle till stars go low,
Having a ball in their nightly show!

A Space Where Wishes Gather

In the corner where socks often flee,
Magic sprinkles, just wait and see.
A spoonful of giggles, a pinch of delight,
We dance like wild owls, hidden from sight.

The chairs become ships sailing to Mars,
With broccoli asteroids and candy bars.
A clock ticks backward, the rules all bend,
In this wacky wonderland, we'll never end.

The Fortress of Starry Night Lullabies

Beneath the blanket, brave knights prepare,
Pillow swords clash in the dreamer's lair.
Candy-coated dragons guard the door,
Silly sheep bounce on the floor.

With giggles like whispers, we take to flight,
Chasing rainbow unicorns into the night.
The tallest tower made of marshmallow,
Who knew slumber could be so hallowed?

The Light of Intangible Hope

A sprinkle of stardust in a cup of tea,
The cat tells secrets only to me.
Footprints in cookies lead to the moon,
What a curious life, as I hum a tune.

Invisible friends share jokes with flair,
They tickle my nose, it's quite the affair.
With laughter echoing in the twilight,
Hope shines brightly, like a kite in flight.

The Voyage Beyond Awakening

In pajamas, we sail on seas,
With breakfast cereal, as the breeze.
A captain made of orange juice,
We navigate with gummy moose.

The winds are whispers, giggles loud,
With stuffed animals as our crowd.
We chart our course through skies of toast,
And steer with laughter, that's the most!

A jellyfish, the friendliest mate,
Spreads sweetness, oh, such a fate!
The ocean swells with bubbles bright,
As we set sail into the night.

With each adventure, a new surprise,
A fruit parade beneath the skies.
Anchors aweigh, we dance and cheer,
Let's sail forever, bring on the cheer!

Flickering Candles of Belief

There's a flicker in the night,
A candle dance, what a sight!
Marshmallows float with great delight,
As shadows play in beams of light.

A secret wish that sings so sweet,
Under the table, I find my feet.
The cake talks back, oh what a treat,
With giggles echoing, we can't be beat!

Balloons in flight, they hide from me,
A wild parade, oh, can't you see?
They float away like dreams that flee,
And yet they make us all so free.

Laughter bubbles, sparks ignite,
Each candle holds a wish tonight.
So blow them out, wish big, believe,
In silliness, we all achieve!

Lanterns in the Labyrinth of Dreams

In a maze made of bright balloons,
We follow trails of silly tunes.
Lanterns giggle, hiding low,
Leading paths where nonsense flows.

A rubber chicken guides the way,
With floppy wings, it wants to play.
Through leafy branches, we take flight,
Chasing shadows, oh what a sight!

With whispers sweet from cookie jars,
We wander far beneath the stars.
Each corner turns with fruitcake trails,
As laughter rings through midnight gales.

We dance through loops, all full of cheer,
In this great maze, there's no fear.
Every twist unveils a dream,
A whimsical, enchanting theme!

Threads of the Night's Embrace

Threads of laughter weave so tight,
In cozy corners, we ignite.
A blanket fort, a hidden space,
Where silly faces fill the place.

Monsters dance with socks on feet,
And pillows bounce in laughing beats.
Under the stars, we share a tale,
Of flying cows with sparkly tails.

Midnight snacks are on the table,
Chocolate rivers, if we're able.
Silly stories twist and twirl,
In the embrace, we laugh and whirl.

With every giggle, joy expands,
A night of whimsy, hand in hands.
As dreams drift softly, we take flight,
In threads of laughter, hearts feel light!

A Canvas of Unfinished Stories

In a world where socks go to hide,
Imagination takes us for a ride.
With crayons dancing on white pages,
Life's funny twists are all the stages.

Cats in capes soar through the air,
While waffles giggle without a care.
Each doodle spins tales so absurd,
Unfinished stories yet to be heard.

A toaster sings in the morning light,
With every pop, it's pure delight.
Jellybeans join in a silly song,
As we all wonder where we belong.

So grab your brush and make a mark,
Let laughter light up the little spark.
For in this canvas, wild and bright,
We craft our dreams with all our might.

Between Realms of Sleep and Wake

In a land where dreams paint the skies,
Pajamas reign with sleepy sighs.
Bears in pajamas have tea at dawn,
While snoozing cats play the ukulele's yawn.

A pillow fight breaks the morning haze,
As chips of laughter fill the days.
Monsters shrink into fluffy throws,
While daydreams dance on timid toes.

Naps are treasures wrapped in smiles,
Each wink unearths a host of wiles.
While coffee mugs hold secrets deep,
In giggles shared before we leap.

So chase the dawn with a silly cheer,
Embrace the whimsy that's ever near.
For in this limbo where dreams collide,
Life's funny joys will surely abide.

The Vault of Hidden Wonders

Behind closed doors, a treasure lies,
Made of giggles and pancake pies.
A jester's hat sits bold and grand,
With flour flying, we take a stand.

The vault is brimming with echoes bright,
Dancing shadows that tickle the night.
Talking mirrors share their charms,
While playful breeze wraps us in arms.

Wind-up toys giggle in grand parades,
And hopscotch fields hold escapades.
Bananas burst forth with tales untold,
In this hidden place where fun unfolds.

So lift the lid and take a peek,
Join the laughter; let joy be sleek.
For in this vault, the magic's real,
Creating wonders that make us squeal.

Twilight's Offering of Epiphanies

As twilight drapes the world in pink,
A sock puppet shares a cup to drink.
Each thought like fireflies takes its flight,
Bubbling ideas spark into the night.

With giggles shared, the stars have fun,
As grumpy clouds begin to run.
A talking moon hums a silly tune,
While dreams unfold beneath its swoon.

In puddles bright, reflections play,
Silly secrets swirl and sway.
The wisdom of frogs on lily pads,
Whispers tales to the curious lads.

So lean back, let those thoughts collide,
In twilight's glow, where wonders bide.
For with each chuckle and bright insight,
We find our joy in this merry night.

Fantasies in the Attic

In the attic, dust bunnies dance,
They twirl and leap, a grand romance.
Old hats wear smiles, quite out of place,
With mismatched socks in a goofy race.

A cat on a shelf dreams of sushi,
While a clock ticks slow, feeling quite pushy.
Jars of pickles hold secrets untold,
As daydreams of pizza start to unfold.

An umbrella sings tunes of the rain,
While a broom complains of life's mundane.
And the old chest, with tales of yore,
Cracks a joke to the floorboards' roar.

So here in this nook, oddities play,
Transforming boredom, in quirky display.
Laughter echoes, no reason to frown,
In this haven where nonsense wears a crown.

The Lullaby of Wishes

A starfish dreams of melting ice cream,
While moonbeams giggle, wishing to beam.
A pillow fights whispers with sleepy thoughts,
As dreams juggle ideas in funny knots.

Umbrellas parade as peacocks in style,
While teacups throw parties, all piled in a pile.
Kites tell their stories in breezy delight,
As bedtime brings laughter to dance through the night.

A fish in pajamas sings off-key,
While fireflies join in, buzzing with glee.
All wishes bounce in a cotton candy world,
Where chuckles and hiccups are freely unfurled.

So close your eyes, let the dreams run wild,
For a night full of laughter, forever beguiled.
In slumber's embrace, mischief prevails,
As wishes reform into giggly tales.

Celestial Hues in the Twilight

In twilight's glow, the moon starts to wink,
A cow takes flight, while the stars start to blink.
Upside-down trees, they wear shoes of clay,
While rivers of lemonade flow away.

Pixies argue over the best bedtime snack,
A toast to the oddities, no reason to crack.
A comet rides by on a roller-coaster,
Dancing to rhythms, becoming a poster.

With paints from the sky, clouds fill with cheer,
As they paint polka-dots on the atmosphere.
Giraffes wear glasses, reading the night,
While squirrels in tuxedos prepare for a flight.

So laugh at the cosmos, so silly and bright,
For twilight brings dreams that tickle with light.
Embrace the absurd, let your heart soar,
In this whimsical world, there's always more.

Cradle of Forgotten Reveries

In the cradle of dreams, a frog plays guitar,
Singing to daisies that stretch from afar.
Moonbeams play hopscotch on jelly bean hills,
While sleepy-eyed owls share snickers and thrills.

A whale in pajamas swims through the air,
Blowing bubble gum, with a whimsical flair.
Crickets in bowties chirp silly refrains,
While wildflower peas dance in bright purple chains.

A teapot sips tea with a rattled old spoon,
And whispers sweet nothings to a cheeky balloon.
In the breeze, all the treasures of youth,
Are tangled in laughter, a colorful truth.

So rock-a-bye giggles, let worries take flight,
In the cradle of reveries, let joy ignite.
For here in the soft, fluffy folds of the night,
Every dream spins a jest, bringing hearts pure delight.

Notes from the Enchanted Space

In a nook where laughter hides,
The sock puppets dance with pride.
A chicken in a bow tie sings,
While a robot juggles shiny rings.

A cat in shades plays chess with mice,
They wager tales of sugar and spice.
The clock ticks backward just for fun,
As they race the setting sun.

A parrot squawks, 'Let's take a trip!'
To sip hot cocoa on a cloud's tip.
Each sip brings giggles to the crew,
As marshmallows swarm like bees, who knew?

The walls are lined with giggle jars,
Each filled with stories of the stars.
In this quirky, silly place,
Reality takes a cheerful chase.

Beneath Pillars of Imagination

Under arches of fluffy dreams,
A jellybean river ceaselessly gleams.
Squirrels in tuxedos throw a ball,
While giraffes gossip, standing tall.

A frog in a top hat croons a tune,
While cupcakes bounce beneath the moon.
Everybody's wearing silly shoes,
Dancing away their morning blues.

The walls say silly things at night,
Like 'Eat dessert before the light!'
Inflatable unicorns take flight,
Sailing through giggles like pure delight.

In this spot, where laughing's prime,
All your woes are lost in rhyme.
With each step, a new joke to unfurl,
In the wacky, wonderful, whimsical world.

Colors of a Fanciful Mind

A canvas where colors speak aloud,
Pink elephants parade, ever proud.
With brushes made of candy canes,
They paint each thought in silly chains.

The sun wears shades, the moon a frown,
As ribbons of laughter dance around.
Every daffodil has a nose ring,
And the clouds can't help but swing.

The trees play hide and seek with glee,
Each whisper of wind's a tickling spree.
Squirrels sport helmets made of cheese,
While the daisies sway in the teasing breeze.

In this realm of absurdity,
Every creature's a celebrity.
They prance and pose in outrageous styles,
Turning mundane moments into smiles.

The Threshold of Visual Poetry

At the edge of a whimsical page,
Doodles and scribbles start to engage.
A worm in glasses composes a rhyme,
While ants juggle seeds, keeping time.

The ink spills stories, full of cheer,
A monkey's dance draws everyone near.
Pencils dream of gliding high,
As words take flight into the sky.

A page of laughter bursts at the seams,
Every character hops like it seems.
On this threshold, nonsense reigns,
Showering joy like springtime rains.

Creativity's winks bring giddy smiles,
As doodles march in funny styles.
At this border of what can be,
Life blooms in thriving hilarity.

Twinkling Thoughts and Moonlit Muses

In the night, socks dance around,
Dreaming of a lost sock found.
A cat debates the stars above,
Should he chase or sit and shove?

Bubbles float like thoughts so light,
They pop with giggles, take to flight.
The moon spills jelly on the ground,
And makes silly sounds that astound.

A bird with glasses sings a tune,
Wonders if fish float with balloons.
The stars all whisper jokes at night,
While shadows play in pure delight.

So laugh along with dreams so bold,
For every thought, a tale retold.
In every giggle, joy is found,
As night wraps us in laughter's sound.

Refuge of the Dreamweaver

In a land of silly chatter,
A toaster dreams of burnt-out batter.
Teapots whistle tunes quite grand,
While slippers try to take a stand.

Umbrellas dance like bumblebees,
Sipping honey from the trees.
Buttons roll and start to play,
Finding joy in every sway.

A rainbow slides from bed to floor,
Inviting us to laugh and roar.
With candy clouds and gummy bears,
We float along without a cares.

So join the fun, don't delay,
In this place where dreams can play.
With giggles sparkling in the air,
We'll weave our dreams with love and care.

View from the Window of Aspirations

Peeking out with eyes so wide,
A squirrel rides a roller slide.
Clouds parade in funny hats,
While raindrops bounce like happy cats.

The sun plays hide and seek with trees,
And tickles flowers in the breeze.
Dandelions wish to take a flight,
Sailing off into the night.

A heartfelt song from crickets plays,
As fireflies join in the craze.
Look closely now, you might just see,
A mouse named Gus with dreams so free.

So open wide that window, dear,
For laughter's echo brings us cheer.
Let aspirations soar and rise,
In this whimsical world, love never dies.

Tapestries of Nighttime Desires

The moon crochets with silver thread,
Stitching wishes in dreams' bed.
A pillow fights with sleepy heads,
While laughter bounces off the spreads.

Stars are cookies for the night,
Each one taking quite a bite.
Mice with hats host a parade,
In moonlit gowns, bright dreams are made.

A wanderer without a care,
Rides a comet through the air.
With every twist, a giggle sounds,
As bedtime stories bounce around.

In this tapestry of fun,
Where every thread is brightly spun.
Let joy weave through the night's embrace,
In dreams' sweet dance, we find our place.

Visions Beneath the Evening Sky

Stars giggle and twinkle with glee,
While I search for a cookie, my best jubilee.
Naps invade my thoughts like a sneaky cat,
Oh, what a world, where the silly things chat!

Moonbeams dance, wearing comical hats,
Whispering secrets to dancing old rats.
With dreams of pizzas that fly in the air,
I laugh so much, I forget my despair!

Clouds turn to shapes of my favorite pies,
Lazing around with spaghetti in the skies.
Balloons tie up my wildest delight,
As I bounce and prance through the sweet starry night!

At the end of this journey, I groan with a grin,
Life's a parade, let the joy bubble in!
With a chuckle I wake, and the laughter stays,
In this realm of whimsy, I'll spend all my days!

The Nest of Silent Longing

In the quiet of night, I search for fun,
Dreaming of pizza and some cake on the run.
A goldfish wears glasses, he's reading a book,
While I try to remember where I left my sock!

A feather floats by, bids the cat a goodnight,
It twirls and it swirls, like a bird in flight.
In the land of sweet wishes, I find my old toy,
A dapper old dinosaur, oh what a joy!

The bed is a cloud, soft as whipped cream,
Each giggle that bubbles makes sleeping a dream.
I catch fireflies sporting tiny bow ties,
As the moon joins the party, to everyone's surprise!

Just when I'm certain I'll float into snooze,
A sock puppet sings a jolly ol' blues.
With a wink and a chuckle, I muse in delight,
Here, amidst laughter, I savor the night!

Tides of the Dreamscape

Sailing on dreams in a boat made of cheese,
The waves say hello with a ticklish breeze.
A walrus in shades shares a joke, quite absurd,
As we drift through a sea of macaroni curds!

Seagulls with sunglasses put on quite a show,
Playing beach volleyball, always ready to go.
I dive with a splash into candy-filled waves,
Where jellyfish giggle, and everyone raves!

A crab wearing socks does the cha-cha with flair,
Surrounded by dolphins who challenge with care.
In this ocean of laughter, nowhere to frown,
I'll spend happily drifting, just spinning around!

As the stars sprinkle cheese on the ocean of mirth,
I gather my dreams, they float with such girth.
With a laugh I awaken, still grinning a beam,
Life's a buffet, filled with whimsy and cream!

The Enchanted Room of Reverie

In a whimsical room where the giggles alight,
Custard waterfalls flow under soft moonlight.
A chair wears a hat, says, "How do you do?"
While the curtains have jokes that they read just to you!

A carpet of marshmallows beneath my bare feet,
Takes me to lands where the silly roam free.
With creatures that chatter in voices so spry,
I can't help but chuckle as they flutter on by!

Walls made of cupcakes, so sweet to the taste,
Every mischievous secret, none of it waste.
A penguin in slippers brews tea with a grin,
As dreams bubble forth like they're made out of whim!

With each hearty laugh, I float higher in glee,
This room is a treasure, a land where we're free.
And as I drift off, with stars winking bright,
I'll carry this laughter into the night!

The Alchemy of Imaginative Dreams

A wizard once brewed a potion,
Made of giggles and joyful motion.
He spilled it all over the floor,
And now the cat dances for more.

A painting began to do a jig,
As the toaster spun around like a twig.
Eggs started singing in the pan,
And toast declared, "I'm a sunny man!"

The broomsticks joined in a conga line,
While the clock chimed in perfect time.
Even the fridge hummed a tune,
In this silly, whimsical afternoon.

So take a chance on your wildest thought,
Mix them up in a pot you've bought.
For life's too short for mundane seams,
Let's all get lost in our quirky dreams!

A Womb of Untold Stories

In a closet, a sock puppet grinned,
Telling tales of the places it's been.
With each knot and every twist,
A sock star would dance, you get the gist.

An old hat nudged a pair of shoes,
"Have you heard the gossip, or just the news?"
Brooms teased mops about their sleek style,
As they shared secrets all the while.

A lunchbox spoke of journeys vast,
Contemplating time and how it passed.
The peeling wallpaper whispered a joke,
As the curtains chuckled, laughter broke.

So gather your items, your treasures rare,
Listen close, for stories fill the air.
From the dustbunnies to the wooden stairs,
In this place, every object cares!

The Keepers of Fleeting Fantasies

In the night, the moon takes a peek,
At the giggles from the rabbit's cheek.
Stars play hide and seek with the sun,
While clouds rumble a tune for fun.

Socks with stripes debated their flair,
About being a fashion statement rare.
A gopher in shades called it art,
While a turtle raced, playing his part.

A dragon in pajamas chased a shrimp,
As ice cream clouds prepared to limp.
This circus of dreams put on a show,
Where fantasy flowed, and giggles would glow.

So let your mind wander and roam,
To where fanciful critters call home.
These keepers of joy, so craftly spun,
Invite you to play until the day's done!

Embracing the Ethereal Whimsy

A talking teapot whistled a cheer,
As pancakes juggled from ear to ear.
Lemonade rain danced down in groove,
While chairs clapped along to the move.

In a bowl of cereal, a fish learned to swim,
As the milk spun around in a whimsical whim.
Each berry burst out in laughter and song,
This breakfast brigade couldn't feel wrong.

An umbrella twirled in a polka dot dress,
While the chimney puffed clouds of happiness.
A toaster winked, "I'm more than just bread,
With dreams of a life beyond being fed!"

So embrace the quirks, the delightfully odd,
Where wild is welcomed; let laughter be a god.
In laughter's embrace, we'll find our way,
To the joyful whims that color our day!

Symphony of Silent Yearnings

In a house made of wishes, so quirky and loud,
The walls have opinions, they're brimming with proud.
Chairs gossip in corners; they're plotting a show,
While socks hold a council; their secrets won't flow.

The cat steals a moment to dance on the floor,
She wears a top hat, and she's begging for more.
The fridge hums a tune, while the cupboard does sway,
This home is a circus, come join in the play!

Under the table, the dust bunnies cheer,
They've thrown a grand party; more guests are so near!
The curtains are laughing, they flutter and sway,
As dreams turn to giggles and lighten the day.

In this hall full of chuckles, where whimsy abounds,
The light bulbs are flickering, making strange sounds.
With a wink and a nod, the world spins around,
In this house of mishaps, laughter's profound!

The Nest of Wandering Minds

In the attic of wonders, strange thoughts start to play,
Where hats masquerade as the sun's bright array.
A teapot is blushing; it's steeping some cheer,
While pages of old books whisper secrets unclear.

The clocks on the wall all tick-tock with a grin,
They race through the hours, and let the fun in.
Beneath the old beams, fairies twirl with delight,
As the kettle boils over from laughter at night.

Couches conspire, they swap stories with pride,
Rug rats are dancing; they've nowhere to hide!
In corners, old sneakers are holding a ball,
As pillows unite for a soft pillow brawl.

So come take a seat and join in with the crew,
In this nest of adventure, there's always room for you.
With giggles as currency and dreams as our guide,
This whimsical space is a journey, not a ride!

Luminescence of the Heart's Desires

The light bulbs are dreaming, they shimmer and glow,
While toasters are boasting about bread they bestow.
A pancake flips forward, a fried egg takes a bow,
In this kitchen of wonders, we toast to the now.

The dishes are chatting, discussing their fate,
And spoons hold a conference, it's getting quite great!
The fridge is a diva, with all the right choices,
While pots tell their stories in grand, raucous voices.

Underneath the table, a snack band takes form,
They're playing with crackers, all crunchy and warm.
The tea kettle whistles a tune just for you,
As dreams turn to feasts and delight in the brew!

So dance through this kitchen, let laughter ignite,
With every small bite, there's a flavor of light.
In this realm of delights, where the silly abide,
Your heart's warmest wishes are never denied!

The Perpetual Daydream

In a room where the ceiling has clouds softly drift,
The shadows are painting with whimsical lift.
A chair spins with glee, it's breaking all rules,
While the ceiling fan chuckles, declaring it's cool.

The windows are winking, they blink with delight,
As the breeze brings a giggle; it's a whimsical flight.
Books wear a jacket of polka-dot fun,
Hiding plots that twist 'til the day is all done.

With sneakers that chatter, and curtains that sway,
The carpet joins in, and it wants to play.
While maps are wandering, searching for paths,
To places that tickle and generate laughs.

In this land of the playful, where daydreams can zoom,
Imagination flourishes, making the room bloom.
So twirl with your thoughts, let your fantasies beam,
For life's little joys are the essence of a dream!

Whispers of the Starry Night

The stars are giggling on high,
They dance like fireflies in the sky.
A cat in pajamas starts to sing,
To every dreamy thing, she's the king.

A moonbeam tickles a lazy dog,
While thunderous snoring shakes the fog.
The owls wear monocles to read,
As hedgehogs debate the latest creed.

Shooting stars are racing by,
One trips and lets out a silly cry.
The night is filled with chuckles and cheers,
As bedtime stories breeze through our ears.

So in this night of laughter and play,
Where fluffy creatures come out to stay.
Let dreams take flight on wings so bright,
As we laugh and twirl 'til the morning light.

Echoes of Forgotten Fantasies

In a land where socks mysteriously roam,
A frog in a tie claims it's his home.
He hops on books, a librarian's plight,
While dragons debate on what's wrong or right.

A toaster pops out a golden knight,
Who proudly proclaims, "It's a toast-filled fight!"
To the couch, they march with great flair,
For pillows are castles, oh what a scare!

The fridge is a portal, or so they say,
With leftovers plotting their escape play.
As forks and spoons join the rebel cheer,
It's a food fight the likes of which we fear!

So let your mind wander, take off your shoes,
With fanciful musings, there's nothing to lose.
In this chaotic dream, we weave and we weave,
Where laughter is gold, and there's always reprieve.

Beneath a Canopy of Hope

Beneath the branches of an old tree,
A squirrel can't grasp his own degree.
He studies hard, but alas, oh dear!
With each turn of the page, he chews on fear.

While ants throw a party, a grand parade,
With tiny balloons and the snacks they've made.
They dance on a leaf, a treetop stage,
With nutty jokes that never age.

A raccoon appears in a top hat so grand,
He juggles three apples, with a wink and a hand.
The moonlight giggles at the silly sight,
As shadows join in the whimsical night.

So come join the fun beneath this green dome,
Where dreams and absurdities call us back home.
In this enchanted grove, laughter runs free,
And every mischief is part of the spree.

Shadows of Midnight Reverie

In the shadows where laughter meets light,
A penguin wears shades and dances with might.
He slides down rainbows, what a cool chap!
Chasing after dreams with a flip and a lap.

A rabbit in slippers invites you to play,
With cupcakes and stories to brighten your day.
They giggle and wiggle as the clock strikes two,
With fairy dust sprinkled in everything they do.

The moon plays hide-and-seek with the clouds,
While shadowy figures make merry crowds.
With invisible ink, they pen jokes galore,
And laughter erupts from the land to the shore.

So if you find yourself late in the night,
With giggles around you, oh hold on tight!
For in this dreamy dance, fun is supreme,
And shadows of joy are woven in a dream.

A Horizon of Sleeping Stars

In the sky, a snoring sun,
Twinkles blink, it's all in fun.
Moonbeams dance like silly cats,
While clouds wear silly hats.

Comets zoom, in haste they race,
Grumpy stars, they hide their face.
Galaxies spin in giggling glee,
While space dust floats like confetti.

A meteor trips and lands with a flop,
Astronauts giggle, they can't stop.
A cosmic party breaks the night,
Where dreams and laughter take their flight.

Sleepy planets find their groove,
In this space where laughter moves.
So drift along, in this bright scene,
With winks and grins, where dreams convene.

The Pinnacle of Uncharted Thoughts

A mountain peak of jumbled ideas,
Where brainwaves frolic, bringing cheers.
Thoughts tumble down like a silly slide,
With giggles echoing far and wide.

Brain cells bounce on trampoline beds,
Silly notions dance in their heads.
Memories juggle like clowns on a stage,
While logic gives in to the whimsy of age.

Exploring paths with wobbly feet,
Every notion is a tasty treat.
Jumbled phrases play hide and seek,
In a carnival of chaos, they speak.

A merry-go-round of quirky plans,
Where dreaming goes on with no demands.
Summit the thoughts, let laughter resound,
In this space, joy can be found.

The Voyage of a Dreamer's Heart

Set sail on a boat made of dreams,
With a jellybean mast, or so it seems.
Waves of whispers tingle and swirl,
As dolphins in tutus begin to twirl.

The compass spins with no direction,
Lost in a sea of pure affection.
Each wave is a giggle, a chuckle, a sigh,
As seagulls wearing sunglasses soar high.

Captain of whimsy, the crew's all aglow,
With treasure maps that barely show.
Each star is a buddy that plays along,
In a quest where silliness is the song.

From islands of laughter to shores of delight,
We sail through a world that's merry and bright.
With each wave crest, let joy impart,
On this glorious ride of a dreamer's heart.

Dreamscapes Beyond the Closed Door

Behind the door, where sillies play,
Dreams tumble out in a comical way.
With a giggle, that quiet creak,
Open the portal, take a peek.

Unicorns in pajamas jump in delight,
While fairies throw confetti at midnight.
A dragon strums on a guitar,
Singing songs from the land of bizarre.

Balloons float by with chatter and cheer,
Whispering jokes for all to hear.
Lollipops grow in colorful trees,
As laughter dances on the breeze.

So step through the entry, leave worries behind,
In this realm where the wacky unwind.
Embrace the absurd, let your spirit soar,
In the dreamscape waiting behind the closed door.

Echoes of Aspirations

In the corner, a gnome does dance,
Wearing socks, he can't take a chance.
He juggles cheese and shouts out loud,
While a cat meows, stealing his crowd.

The ceiling fan spins a wild tale,
Of superhero ants that never fail.
They save the day with a crumb or two,
While the dog just snores, dreaming of stew.

A wishbone whispers, 'Pick me, pick me!'
But the goldfish just swirls in glee.
With feathered hats and oversized shoes,
Each day's a party, with nothing to lose.

The echoes of hopes twist and twine,
In this whimsical world, all is divine.
As laughter lifts, like bubbles in air,
Every moment holds a joyful flair.

Sanctuary of the Imagination

The walls are covered in scribbled dreams,
Where unicorns prance in sunlit beams.
A pillow fort wears a crown of curls,
While the cat conducts tiny marching pearls.

Inside this realm, a soup can sings,
Of pirate ships and rubber band slings.
A jellybean wizard waves his wand,
While the floor is a sea; adventure is planned.

The shadows dance as the night sneaks in,
With magical creatures ready to spin.
The old clock winks, and time takes a break,
Together we laugh until we quake.

In this sanctuary, nothing's too wild,
Imagination's the heart of the child.
So grab your dreams, let's ride on a whale,
Together, we'll forge an epic tale.

Dreams Drift on Silver Clouds

On cotton candy clouds, we float and sigh,
With marshmallow pillows piled sweet and high.
Balloons filled with giggles float away,
Chasing rainbows in the light of day.

A dragon bakes cookies in the sky,
While a kite-shaped squirrel gives it a try.
With cupcakes and sprinkles tumbling about,
Each bite brings laughter — there's never a doubt.

The stars wink down, sharing secret jokes,
As moonbeams dance with giggly folks.
In dreamy attire, we twirl and leap,
Making magic from starlight, far from sleep.

While dandelions whisper, "Make a wish,"
A bubble bath party is the ultimate dish.
Floating on laughter, we chase after light,
In this dreamland, where all is bright.

The Realm Beyond the Ceiling

Beyond the ceiling, the socks come alive,
With mustaches made from a brush and a jive.
They dance with the curtains, a waltz of delight,
While dust bunnies giggle, shivering with fright.

The chandelier twinkles with fairy-like glee,
As the coffee pot whistles a jazzy decree.
The bookshelf erupts in a story of pies,
With plot twists that leave you rolling with cries.

A raccoon wears glasses, reading aloud,
While rain boots tap dance to the tunes of the crowd.
The rubber chicken leads a comedy night,
Where punchlines are shot from a pillow's soft height.

With echoes of laughter, the room spins around,
This whimsical kingdom where silliness found.
So gather your giggles, let's broaden our scope,
For in this realm, we find laughter and hope.

Journey to the Heart of Dreams

On a quest for treasure, I took a ride,
Found a giant squirrel, my trusty guide.
We danced on clouds, oh what a sight,
    Wearing pajamas, feeling light.

A unicorn popped up, spilled my tea,
Said, "Is this the place to be carefree?"
    I laughed so hard, I lost my hat,
    Chased it down with a silly cat.

A rainbow slid by, it winked and sighed,
"Where's the gold?" I asked, feeling pride.
It giggled and danced, then lost its way,
In a fountain of chocolate, sweetly astray.

In this land of odd, dreams come alive,
Each giggle and gaffe helps you thrive.
We took a snapshot, all full of cheer,
Who knew dreaming could be so dear?

The Mirage of Delight

A flying fish sang songs of delight,
While a cactus wore sunglasses, what a sight!
They invited me in for a picnic feast,
With jellybeans and rainbows, at least.

I sipped from a cup made of cloud,
A melty ice cream, they all cheered loud.
The elephant danced in polka dot shoes,
While fortune cookies shared my good news.

A goat in a tuxedo just missed the fun,
Tripped on his bowtie—it weighed a ton!
Laughter erupted, it echoed all day,
In the mirage, worries went far away.

So, join the madness, don't hide your grin,
In the midst of silly, let joy begin.
For in this strange world, laughter is king,
A mirage of delights, come on and sing!

A Nest for the Wandering Spirit

In a twisted tree, a nest made of dreams,
Sat a parrot who spoke in rhymes and schemes.
"What brings you here to my cozy retreat?"
She offered me snacks—sour candy, quite sweet.

A raccoon with sass was polishing shoes,
"Here, take a pair, but they'll give you the blues!"
I slipped them on, they squeaked with a bounce,
As I wobbled and tumbled, just like a flounce.

A party of socks held a grand little dance,
Mismatched and merry; they took every chance.
The dancing was wild, everyone was a hit,
Who knew such fun in a sock could exist?

So gather your dreams, come strut with the crowd,
In a nest where oddballs are humorously loud.
Here spirits wander, and giggles take flight,
In the nest of the quirky, all feels just right!

Celestial Threads of Yearning

Stars tangled up with a fruitcake delight,
Couldn't tell if it was day or night.
A comet zoomed by with a wink and a grin,
"Have you heard? The moon's wearing thin!"

Marshmallows bounced on twinkling beams,
They whispered soft secrets and wild dreams.
While a feline on Mars played chess in space,
Pausing only to groom his furry face.

Galaxies giggled, light years away,
As comets spun tales of a golden hay.
They warned me to watch for the meteor showers,
"They burst with surprises and mysterious powers!"

So let's weave our dreams with shimmering threads,
Imagination blooms where laughter spreads.
In the cosmos of chuckles, we'll twirl and play,
Celestial joy carries us far away!

The Archway to Imagination

Through a door of candy canes,
Where socks fly like balloons,
I'm king of my domain,
With pet unicorns and raccoons.

Underneath the jelly trees,
I dance like silly bread,
In a world of giggle bees,
Where cupcakes earn their spread.

Coloring the skies with cheese,
And clouds made of cotton cake,
I climb hills of jelly peas,
In a world on an upside break.

With dreams that hop on pogo sticks,
And rainbows shaped like spoons,
I ride the waves of goofy tricks,
In a land of laughing tunes.

Skylit Visions in Slumber

In dreamland of rubber ducks,
I sail on boats made of bread,
Where ice cream rains and laughter plucks,
Every thought fills my head.

I juggle ants in a top hat,
And wear shoes that squeak with glee,
Talk to fish, and chat with cats,
In a whirlpool of jubilee.

With pillows morphing into planes,
I fly to shores of jellybeans,
Where clouds dissolve with silly stains,
And tickle-fights are routine scenes.

As stars play hide and seek at night,
My dreams pirouette around,
With giggles echoing in flight,
In a world of joy found.

Nestled Amongst Celestial Hopes

Beneath a tree of scribbled stars,
I wear pajamas made of cheese,
And zip through galaxies in cars,
That toast and say, "Oh, yes please!"

With marshmallow clouds as my bed,
I bounce on moons made of marsh,
Where dancing fruits do tango red,
And laughter's always on a lark.

I sip from cups of fizzy dreams,
And ride rainbows down the hill,
Where friendly monsters plot and scheme,
To bake me cakes that give a thrill.

My pillow whispers jokes at night,
And blankets join in on the fun,
In a land of giggles and light,
Where dreams and sillies run.

The Sanctuary of Wishes

In a fort made of silk and gold,
I wish for cookies that can dance,
With lemonade that sings out bold,
And cupcakes in a bubble trance.

The time flies fast on Wishing Wheels,
As I craft dreams with silly glue,
Each thought a carrot that reveals,
A world where oddities ensue.

With crayons sprouting from the ground,
I color in the beams of light,
Where silly monsters twirl around,
And everyone is dressed just right.

As wishes bounce on pogo sticks,
And laughter fills the air so bright,
I dream of magic, munch and mix,
In this sanctuary of delight.

Starlit Pathways of Yearning

In a world where socks go astray,
I've lost more than just my way.
The moonlight calls, with a cheeky grin,
Let the lost adventures now begin!

A hat that dances on a cat,
Who knows where it's at – oh, imagine that!
With a giggle and a jump, we'll find our tune,
Toe-tapping under the light of the moon.

Chasing shadows that tickle our toes,
Finding secrets where laughter grows.
A rocket made of paper and string,
Launching dreams into the sky, we'll sing!

So let's waltz past the stars so bright,
With hiccups of joy, we'll dance all night.
The pathway calls, let's go explore,
Where dreams are wild and spirits soar!

The Attic of Forgotten Dreams

In a dusty nook where treasures hide,
There's a giraffe that wears a tie so wide.
A telephone built for cheeky chats,
Ringing up friends – or maybe just cats!

Old board games with laughter trapped,
Snakes and ladders that never mapped.
Dart boards filled with pies and cakes,
Here, only joy, and no heartbreaks!

A hat rack sings a silly tune,
With floppy hats that make us swoon.
Under a blanket, we start to scheme,
To travel places that glow and beam.

So join me here, where time stands still,
In this attic of fun – what a thrill!
With a giggle and a hop, let's take a chance,
For in these dreams, we will dance!

Cradled in the Arms of Imagination

On a swing made of candy and beams,
We'll soar through the air, lost in dreams.
Let's paddle our boats made of chocolate pie,
With jellyfish jumping as the clouds fly by.

A land where bananas wear shoes of red,
And the grass tickles us in our bed.
Pets who talk and dance on a dime,
Every moment here is simply sublime.

With bubblegum rain that pops overhead,
We'll chase after giggles that never tread.
Every giggle is a spark of zeal,
In this wacky land, we always feel!

So come take my hand; let's spin and twirl,
In the lands of make-believe, give it a whirl!
Where imagination blooms without any care,
With laughter and dreams, we'll dance in the air!

A Cocoon of Tomorrow's Hope

In a bubble where tomorrow gleams,
We're building castles, crafting dreams.
With marshmallow bricks, we'll raise the walls,
Elastic lounging — answering the calls!

Chasing rainbows that mean believe,
Each step we take, new fun to weave.
Dancing on clouds made of fluffy cream,
In this laughter bubble, all is a dream!

A trampoline of hope springs us high,
With swings of joy reaching the sky.
Every wish we whisper takes flight,
In a cozy nook, all feels just right.

So let's wrap our joys in this fluffy space,
Creating tomorrows at a carefree pace.
With giggles and smiles, we rise like a kite,
In our cocoon of hope, everything's bright!

A Fortress of Quiet Desires

In a castle made of pillows, so soft and bright,
Lies a knight with pajamas, ready for the night.
He battles dreams of snacks, warriors of ice cream,
With a shield of good intentions, he reigns supreme.

His trusty steed is a cat, with a crown of fluff,
Together they venture, but it's always too rough.
When the dragon of reality starts to bug,
He pulls out his blanket for a snug little hug.

The jesters are giggling, in the corner they hide,
As he juggles his wishes, feeling silly with pride.
They tickle his fancies, then dart away fast,
Leaving our knight wondering how long dreams last.

But fear not, dear friend, for the laughter is light,
In this fortress of joy, everything feels right.
With the moon as his lantern, and stars as his charts,
He sails 'cross his thoughts with a basket of hearts.

The Dreamweaver's Corner

In a cozy little nook, where giggles abound,
A squirrel with a hat shares secrets profound.
He weaves together wishes from the fluffiest thread,
Creating a tapestry of dreams in your head.

The moon winks at him, with a sparkle so bright,
As he spins tales that dance like moths in the night.
With a twirl and a giggle, they flit through the air,
In the Dreamweaver's Corner, all worries are rare.

A cloud floats by with a message of cheer,
Reminding each dreamer that magic is near.
With marshmallow friends, they sip cocoa with glee,
Every thought is a party, come join the spree!

The clock ticks around, but time holds its breath,
In this corner of joy, there's no fear of death.
With a chorus of laughter, dreams come alive,
In the weaver's embrace, all wishes can thrive.

Where Hopes Take Anchor

On a ship of bright colors, hopes sail the sea,
With anchors of laughter, they're happy and free.
As seagulls of dreams swoop and dive all around,
Each wish finds a haven, a fun-loving sound.

The captain wears socks that don't seem to match,
With a map made of giggles, he'll never detach.
He charts out a course through the laughter-filled waves,
In this sea of ideas, fortune always saves.

The fish tell no tales, they're too busy to chat,
While the octopus juggles his bright, silly hat.
They dance with the bubbles, in a splish-splashing tune,
While the sun gives a wink, wishing dreams overmoon.

Where hopes take their anchor, fun's never amiss,
In a world where each wave brings a playful kiss.
So hoist up your sails, let your spirit take flight,
In this ship of good fortune, all is delight.

Flickers of the Unseen Realm

In a realm full of giggles, where shadows can play,
The flickers of laughter light up every day.
A monster with socks that are lovingly tossed,
Makes friends with the echoes of dreams that were lost.

Here, colors are playful, with tricks up their sleeves,
As wishes run wild, dancing through rustling leaves.
The star-winks are silly, with grins that are wide,
In the unseen realm, there's no need to hide.

Each flicker a promise of giggles to come,
With a drum made of marshmallows, together they hum.
The fairies all flit with a wink and a whirl,
Spreading whispers of joy, in a sprightly swirl.

In this unseen tapestry, fun thrives every night,
With shadows that giggle, and dreams taking flight.
Each flicker a treasure, a spark in the dark,
In a world of pure joy, where laughter leaves a mark.

Beneath Shelters of Hope

In the attic, the cat wears a hat,
Sipping tea with a talking rat.
Bicycles race without any brakes,
They giggle and wobble till someone quakes.

A toaster debates with a blender in fun,
Arguing if toast should be done in the sun.
While shoes have a dance off, all laced up tight,
Spinning and twirling till they fade from sight.

A bear grips a donut, eyeing the fridge,
As if it were gold, all sparkling and big.
Under the smiles of this cheerful spree,
What wonders unfold—come join with me!

At dusk, the chairs hold a raucous debate,
Who's the best dancer and knows how to skate.
The ceiling fans spin tales, oh what a sight,
In a realm where the funny worlds ignite.

A Tapestry of Illusions

In the corners where shadows play peek-a-boo,
A fox paints the walls with bright colors too.
Jellybeans sway with a musical twist,
As each note makes the wallpaper do flips.

A cloud spun from laughter drifts through the air,
With umbrellas dancing without any care.
The moon wears pajamas, adorned with stars,
While sunbeams hopscotch over old cars.

A garden of gnomes throws a wild parade,
As dandelions join with a grand charade.
Socks switch partners, then take to the floor,
This fabric of fun holds forevermore!

'Til dawn whispers gently, "Let's do it again!"
A world made of giggles, where nonsense meets zen.
Beneath colors vibrant, life bursts at the seams,
In this place of peculiar yet perfect dreams.

Shadows in the Twilight Corner

In twilight's embrace, the shadows conspire,
To start a game of jump rope with fire.
A broom takes a ride on the back of a snail,
While frogs in tuxedos recount their last tale.

The clock's ticking laughter echoes in time,
As squirrels juggle nuts, perfectly prime.
A pizza slice dresses up like a king,
Ruling over crusts with a rubber band ring.

Cushions debate which one is more soft,
While gridiron dreams let the pillow fort loft.
Every flip of the hourglass brings a loud cheer,
From whispers of mischief that bubble near.

As night deepens gently with a winky wink,
The world joins the party to giggle and think.
In this space of absurdity, joy finds a seam,
The essence of laughter, oh what a dream!

Night's Embrace of Possibility

When bedtime stories become quite alive,
A giraffe rolls dice, trying to survive.
Dinosaurs dance on the edge of a bed,
While candy bars plot to take over the spread.

The moon sings a tune, all sparkles and glee,
While shadows in glasses sip herbal tea.
Zebras striped in pajamas play cards till dawn,
In a match of who snores like a booming brawn.

A parade of stars rush, twinkling in lines,
Crafting sleeping bag castles made from designs.
As slippers converse about comfort and warmth,
The extra-large teddy bears lead a grand swarm.

In this nighttime whimsy, adventures unfold,
With dreams where the laughter is never too bold.
So raise up the curtains, let the fun flow free,
In worlds of delight, come join and just be!

The Hidden Gallery of the Heart

In a room where laughter hides,
Framed memories dance like silly tides.
A sock on the wall, a hat on the floor,
Tipsy portraits whisper, 'Come see more!'

The heart has a brush that's comically keen,
Painting dreams of cats dressed as queens.
Whimsical scenes of pie in the sky,
Where everyone munches while floating by.

A sneezing giraffe, a ticklish tree,
With butterflies that giggle in glee.
Each canvas a chuckle, each hue a smile,
A gallery made for the whimsies that pile.

So step inside this colorful room,
Where even the shadows dance and bloom.
With a wink and a quirk, nothing's too absurd,
In this hidden gallery, laughter's the word.

Journeys in the Realm of Possibility

With a compass made of jellybeans,
I sail on boats of marshmallow dreams.
Tacky maps draw paths through candy trees,
Where laughter floats upon the breeze.

Exploring lands where socks fly free,
On trampoline clouds, just you and me.
Sipping soda from a rainbow stream,
In this realm, all is a whimsical scheme.

Clouds wear pajamas, stars play chess,
Frogs in tuxedos look quite the mess.
Every turn brings a giggle and glee,
Where every odd notion can truly be.

So take that leap, let silliness flow,
In this curious land where daydreams grow.
You never know where the laughter will lead,
Just follow your heart, it's all that you need.

Parables of the Sleeping Mind

In the land of nod, odd things appear,
A couch that can talk and a cat that can steer.
Singing pillows and blankets that dance,
With giggles erupting at every chance.

The clock is a chicken, clucking with pride,
Time's just a joke on this zany ride.
With dreams wearing boots and tutus galore,
Every snooze is an open door.

Monkeys in bow ties, sipping sweet tea,
Tell tales of socks lost in the spree.
Each snore is a chorus, each yawn a song,
In this wacky world where we all belong.

So dream without limits, laugh without care,
For every wild thought is floating in air.
With sleepy eyes crinkling and spirits so light,
These parables thrive in the heart of the night.

Gates to the Hall of Whispers

Beyond the gates where secrets play,
Lively echoes dance in a quirky ballet.
Whispers of cookies and lemonade sounds,
Where giggles pop up like bubbling hounds.

Walls that murmur silly little rhymes,
Tickling your ears with wobbly chimes.
A jester's cap spins tales of delight,
Turning shadows into laughter at night.

Visit the corners where giggles reside,
With secret passageways and silly slides.
In every nook, a jolly surprise,
Where laughter ignites like fireflies.

So wander through these gates, take a peek,
In the hall of whispers, it's funny you seek.
Embrace every chuckle, let joy be your guide,
In the essence of laughter, let your heart glide.

The Promised Land of Fantasia

In a land where socks come alive,
They dance in pairs to jive and thrive.
Pants that talk, and shirts that sing,
A wardrobe that offers a funny fling.

Where pickles wear top hats with flair,
And jellybeans surf the air.
Tea cups toss chocolate chips with glee,
A salad sings, 'You can't catch me!'

In this world of giggles and cheer,
Where bananas roller skate, oh dear!
Cabbages make silly jokes at noon,
And pizzas burst out in a funky tune.

So come on in, leave worries behind,
In this joyous place, fun's redefined.
With every step, let laughter bloom,
In a realm where silliness finds room.

Glimmers of Unspoken Wishes

On a cloud where wishes are made,
A talking cat is the parade.
He juggles stars with a quirky grin,
And hula hoops made of lemon skin.

Rainbows sprout up like candy canes,
While marshmallow clouds bring silly gains.
A sneezing giant tickles the sky,
And rubber ducks begin to fly.

Dreams twirl in a whimsical dance,
Feathers and glitter lead the prance.
Frogs do the cha-cha with delight,
While moonbeams giggle through the night.

So wish a little louder, my friend,
In this land where laughter won't end.
With each chuckle, a new tale we'll weave,
In a place that's hard to believe.

The Architect of Fantasies

In a realm where dreams sketch the night,
An architect builds with pure delight.
He uses giggles to craft a door,
And laughter becomes the key to explore.

With a blueprint of balloons in the air,
He constructs silly towers without a care.
Where sippy cups spill tales from the past,
And the walls stick to truth, but not too fast.

Gummy bears help with the heavy load,
While crayons dance down the rainbow road.
Paintbrushes tickle as they paint the blue,
In this funny playground, all wishes come true.

So come and build your dreams as you please,
With each silly step, feel the breeze.
In the land of imagination's might,
Where every day starts with delight.

The Chamber of Secrets and Dreams

Behind a door marked with a grin,
Lies a chamber where peculiar begins.
A closet of sock puppets in disguise,
And a bookshelf that whispers surprise.

Math books break into hearty laughter,
While history scrolls dance happily after.
Spoons debate on who stirs best,
While forks perform in a silly fest.

In this chamber, time takes a pause,
As cupcakes debate their glorious cause.
With a ping pong table made of jelly,
Every heartbeat brings smiles and belly.

So sneak a peek, if you dare,
In this world full of whimsical flair.
Secrets await, just follow the stream,
In the chamber where wackiness is the dream.

The Canvas of the Cosmic Mind

A brush dipped in laughter, strokes all around,
Kaleidoscope visions where giggles abound.
With planets in pajamas and stars on a spree,
Even comets can't help but chuckle with glee.

Aliens dance while sipping on tea,
Drawing constellations with a wink, full of glee.
A rocket that snores, a moon that can wink,
Who knew the cosmos had humor to think?

Saturn spins laughing in its rings made of pie,
While Mars tries to prank, oh, give it a try!
In this funny realm where silliness gleams,
Every corner hides whispers and beams.

So grab all your dreams and paint them like art,
In this cosmic comedy, pure joy plays a part.
The stars shine in laughter, a giggling parade,
Come join in the fun, let's not be afraid!

Melodies of the Dreamer's Lament.

In the land of lost socks where mismatched dreams roam,
A serenade echoes, calling minds back home.
The piano plays loudly, but it's slightly off-key,
As dancing cats croon their own melody.

A hat made of feathers, a shoe on a cat,
Compose such a symphony, imagine that!
The moon joins the chorus with a chuckle or two,
While echoing stars laugh at all that we do.

A jester of somnolence, juggling with flair,
Dances on dreams with no worry or care.
With twilight as chorus, the night hums along,
Each giggle and sigh builds the whimsical song.

So let's sip on our wishes like tea brewed with fun,
And jam with our dreams 'til the rising of sun.
In this humorous lament, we'll giggle and sway,
For melodies linger, in laughter, they play!

Whispers of the Midnight Sky

Secrets twirl up in the air like a kite,
As owls hold a conference on who's wrong or right.
The stars spin their tales while the crickets all groan,
As moths give advice in a soft, silver tone.

A squirrel in pajamas devises a plan,
To steal all the dreams of the sleepiest man.
While the moon tries to whisper with charm and allure,
But stumbles on jokes that are not so demure.

The clouds wear their pillows, fluffing them high,
While raindrops debate if they should even cry.
With comets cracking jokes, the night giggles sweet,
As everyone joins in to tap dance on feet.

So join in the whispers that float in the breeze,
For even the night sky knows how to tease.
With laughter and joy, let silliness fly,
Beneath the blanket of this midnight sky!

Beneath the Starlit Canopy

In a field of bright daisies, we gather for fun,
With fireflies joining, their glow never done.
The moon is our spotlight, it beams with a grin,
As frogs sing like rock stars, let the laughter begin!

A picnic of nonsense, full of jellybean stew,
Odd marshmallow dreams and a rainbow or two.
The ants hold a dance, with disco balls spun,
While squirrels serve popcorn—we're never outdone!

Galaxies cheer as we play tag with the breeze,
While shooting stars giggle, dropping laughs with ease.
Oh, what a gathering, where dreams clap and cheer,
Beneath the bright canopy, our joys reappear!

So raise up your voice, let your spirits all soar,
In this world made of laughter, there's always more.
With giggles and dreams wrapped up all through the night,
Let's dance 'neath the starlight, a whimsical sight!

An Odyssey of Thoughts and Wishes

In a castle made of fluffy clouds,
A knight snores, wearing pink pajamas.
His dreams are filled with giant cows,
Who sing and dance like rockstar llamas.

A dragon brews his morning tea,
While fairies play a game of chess.
Each move is met with raucous glee,
And every loss means wearing a dress!

A pirate sails on streams of cream,
With chocolate gold piled by his side.
He shouts, 'Arrr, the finest dream!'
As jellybeans become the tide.

Beneath the swirling, giggling sun,
A cactus wears a party hat.
With laughter loud, the day is won,
As socks escape to chase a cat!

The Hideaway of Aspirations

In a nook where wishes hide away,
A mouse speaks fluent French and fun.
He dreams of cheese that sings all day,
And dances 'round just like a bun.

A tape dispenser starts to sing,
To sticky notes that float like stars.
With paper planes, they take to wing,
And fly to Mars in candy cars.

A lizard dons a fancy hat,
And juggles jelly, just for kicks.
He earns a laugh, imagine that!
While ants perform their quirky tricks.

In the corner, dreams collide,
As laughter fills the summer air.
For every wish, a joy to bide,
And memories are held with care.

Serenity of the Starlit Veil

With purple nights and blue delight,
A sleepwalker dances on the moon.
He bows to stars, not feeling slight,
While crickets play a jazzy tune.

A ladybug wears fairy wings,
Reciting tales of lazy bees.
She twirls around and softly sings,
While sipping dew from magic trees.

A squirrel juggles acorns bold,
As owls hoot wisdom from their thrones.
They share the secrets of the old,
While counting all their funny bones.

Beneath the twinkling whirls of night,
Dreams wander free, a joyful spree.
For who would trade a giggle's flight,
For solemn sighs—no, not for me!

Tales from the Whispering Eaves

Here's a tale from shadows deep,
Where broomsticks play, and owls bake pie.
They stir the night as others sleep,
With chocolate chips that touch the sky.

A ghost who loves to play charades,
Throws cushions high and laughs out loud.
He's mastered all the silly trades,
Inviting owls to join the crowd.

An elf once brewed a magic stew,
That turned a frog into a prince.
And every time he yelled out, 'Boo!'
The kitchen danced and laughed a wince.

Each corner holds a secret jest,
With echoes of a giggling breeze.
In this place, we find our best,
Embracing life with boundless ease.

The Garden of Unbounded Thoughts

In a garden where thoughts run free,
A snail wears a hat and sings off-key.
The daisies dance in silly delight,
While clouds giggle softly, hiding from sight.

A frog plays chess with a bumblebee,
Knocking over pawns with sheer glee.
The sun winks down, a playful light,
As flowers debate who's the most bright.

They share their secrets, wild and grand,
Piled high on a fussy mushroom stand.
"Is this the best tea?" an owl quips bold,
While squirrels sip acorn brew, uncontrolled.

At dusk comes a cat in a polka-dot tie,
Proposing a toast to the starry sky.
The garden buzzes with laughter distinct,
In the chaos of thoughts, magic is linked.

Within Invisible Boundaries

Within walls drawn by none but a pup,
A furniture fort holds a grand sup.
A couch potato rules with a remote,
While cats plot a coup on a fuzzy boat.

Invisible lines keep the snacks in place,
As silly masks wear a beatific face.
The goldfish dreams big in a bowl of glass,
Whispers to crayons of the heart's wild class.

A rubber ducky quacks at the moon,
Finding a rhythm to a nonsensical tune.
Its quack echoes loudly, a clarion call,
In this space made of laughter, there's plenty for all.

Gerbils in capes are ready to race,
Twirling in circles with style and grace.
Together they leap, with purpose profound,
Crafting a maze that knows no bound.

Echoing Silence of Illusions

In a room where whispers do somersaults,
Dreams play hopscotch, avoiding the faults.
A chair claims it's king, but it wobbles like mad,
While shadows break-dance, making it glad.

A clock ticks backward, much to its glee,
Telling tales of what used to be.
But who listens close to a ticking sound?
When umbrella parrots give wisdom profound?

Chairs hold meetings, the agenda? To nap,
While the curtains weave stories in a flap.
The rug spins yarns of curious dreams,
As socks conspire with echoes and beams.

Time takes a breather, and laughter intrudes,
Filling the silence with playful moods.
Invisible threads tying it all,
In this room of nonsense, there's never a fall.

Where the Wild Things Dream

Where wild things frolic in whimsical fun,
Pigs wear sunglasses, basking in the sun.
A fox on a skateboard performs a flip,
While frogs flip-flop on a chocolate chip.

Unicorns froth up sparkling soda streams,
And ride on the backs of bouncing moonbeams.
Hedgehogs strum banjos while critters jig,
In a dance that feels like a candy gig.

A porcupine juggles pickles with flair,
Squealing with laughter, a rollicking air.
Overhead, a parrot with tales to share,
Throws confetti of dreams, drifting everywhere.

At twilight, the moon throws a party for all,
Where wild things gather to sing and to sprawl.
In a world unfettered, they find their own way,
Creating a ruckus until light of day.

www.ingramcontent.com/pod-product-compliance
Lightning Source LLC
Chambersburg PA
CBHW060112230426
43661CB00003B/164